RACE TO THE BOTTOM OF THE OCEAN

BY GRETCHEN MAURER

Momentum

Published by The Child's World®
1980 Lookout Drive • Mankato, MN 56003-1705
800-599-READ • www.childsworld.com

Photographs ©: National Geographic/Album/
Newscom, cover, 1, 6; World History Archive/
Newscom, 5; Shutterstock Images, 9, 18; Kathy
Hutchins/Shutterstock Images, 10; AP Images,
13; Janelle Lugge/iStockphoto, 14; Saeed Khan/
AFP/Getty Images, 16, 22; Willy Sanjuan/Invision/
AP Images, 21; NOAA Office of Ocean Exploration
and Research, 24; Red Line Editorial, 25; Saul
Loeb/AFP/Getty Images, 26; Solodov Aleksei/
Shutterstock Images, 28

Copyright © 2020 by The Child's World®
All rights reserved. No part of this book may be
reproduced or utilized in any form or by any means
without written permission from the publisher.

ISBN 9781503832244
LCCN 2018962833

Printed in the United States of America
PA02421

ABOUT THE AUTHOR

Gretchen Maurer is the author of several books for young readers. Gretchen's writings have also been published in magazines such as *Highlights for Children* and *Adventure Cyclist*. She lives in Northern California with her family.

CONTENTS

FAST FACTS 4

CHAPTER ONE
"Cut It Away" 7

CHAPTER TWO
Teamwork 11

CHAPTER THREE
A Race for Time 15

CHAPTER FOUR
The Big Dive 19

CHAPTER FIVE
The Journey Continues 27

Think About It 29
Glossary 30
Source Notes 31
To Learn More 32
Index 32

MOMENTUM

FAST FACTS

What Is the Challenger Deep?
▶ The Challenger Deep is the deepest point on Earth's surface. It is in the Mariana Trench in the Pacific Ocean.

▶ The Challenger Deep is 36,037 feet (10,984 m) deep. That is nearly 1 mile (1.6 km) deeper than the height of Mount Everest.

Information About the Area
▶ The water pressure at the bottom of the Challenger Deep is nearly 1,000 times the pressure at sea level. The pressure is equal to that of 50 jumbo jets on top of a person's head.

▶ The deepest a fish has ever been spotted was at 26,715 feet (8,142 m). The water pressure becomes too intense below that for fish and many other creatures to form bones.

Journeys to the Bottom
▶ James Cameron's *Deepsea Challenger* sub is 24 feet (7.3 m) long, about the size of a limousine.

▶ Only two other people besides Cameron piloted a sub to the bottom of the Challenger Deep: Jacques Piccard and Don Walsh. They went down in the *Trieste* in 1960.

One feature in the Mariana Trench is ▶ vents that release carbon dioxide.

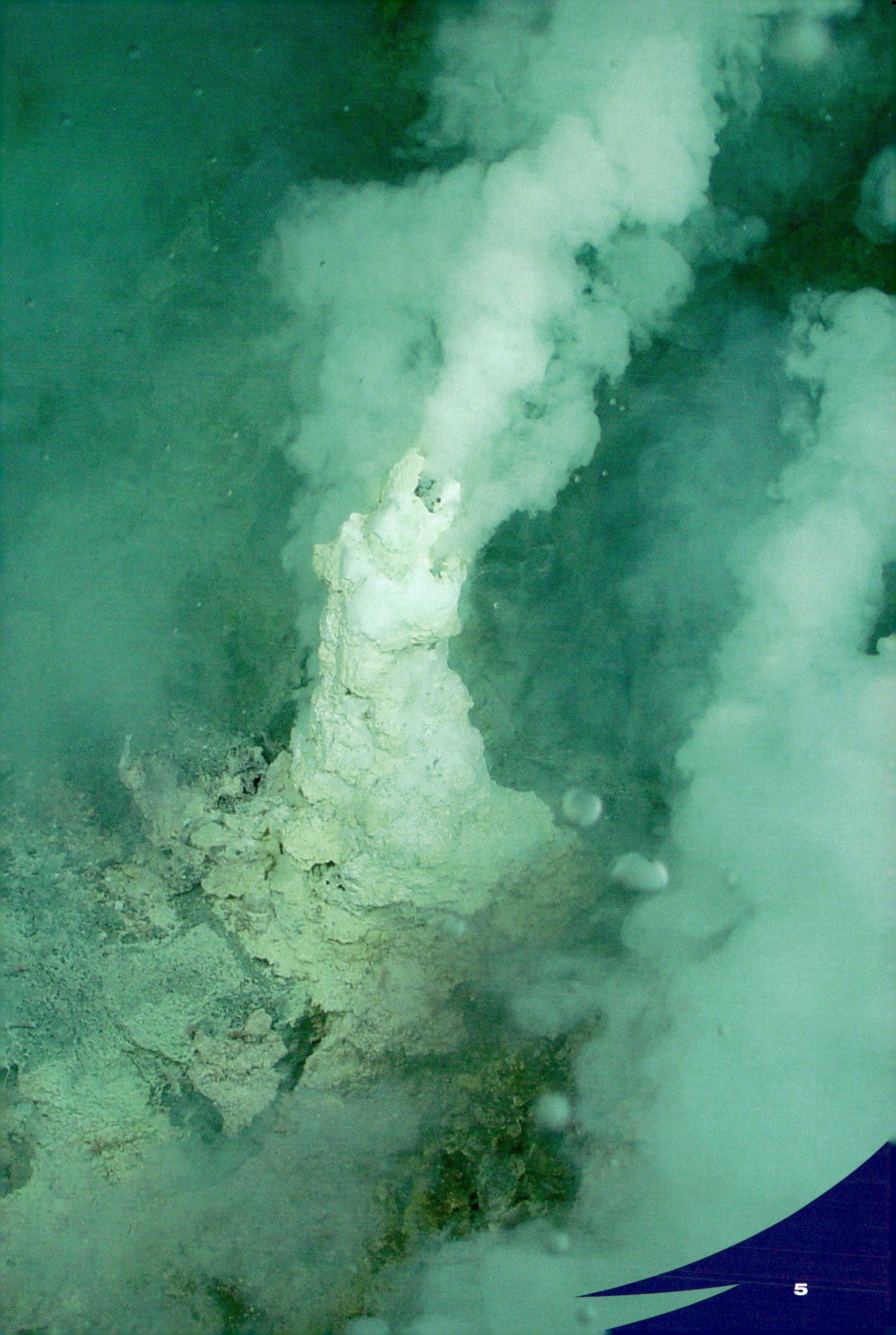

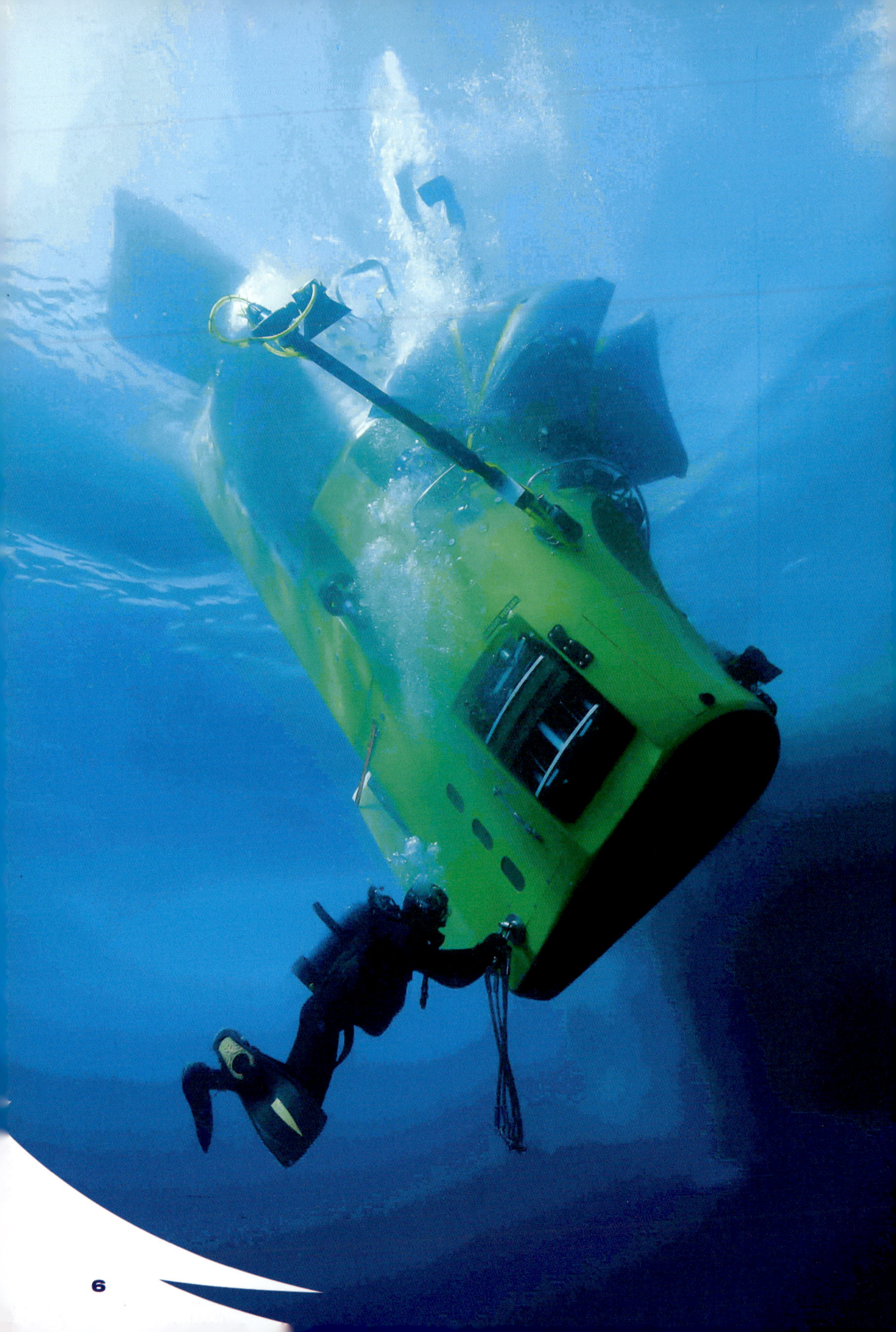

CHAPTER ONE

"CUT IT AWAY"

On March 26, 2012, the wind whipped the Pacific Ocean into a frenzy. James Cameron, a filmmaker and ocean explorer, squeezed into the pilot **sphere** of his lime green sub, the *Deepsea Challenger*. The sub tossed and turned in the massive ocean waves. Cameron's support team watched anxiously from the deck of the launch ship. Cameron was ready to become the first solo pilot ever to reach the deepest part of the Pacific Ocean's Mariana Trench—the Challenger Deep.

For more than seven years, Cameron had carefully considered all that could go wrong with this dive. For example, the 43-inch (109-cm) wide pilot sphere could cave in from the crushing water pressure. If that happened, he could die immediately. Also, the electrical gadgets could burst into flames and he'd have to spray them with a fire extinguisher.

◄ The *Deepsea Challenger* was tested many times before James Cameron made his dive into the Challenger Deep.

The weights could fail to eject when he flipped the switch to come back to the surface, and he could be stuck at the bottom of the ocean and freeze.

But in that moment, right before Cameron gave the command to release the sub from the flotation devices, he felt calm. He trusted the thousands of hours of work he and his engineers had put into developing his cutting-edge sub. He was curious about what he'd see in the deepest part of the ocean, nearly 7 miles (11 km) below the surface. Would he discover unknown giant creatures? Bizarre rock formations?

Just before the *Deepsea Challenger* sank below the churning surface, Cameron noticed that a hatch had popped open.

WHAT'S IN THE TRENCH?

The Mariana Trench is near Guam, a U.S. territory. The trench is 120 times larger than the Grand Canyon. President George W. Bush established a national monument in 2009 to protect this unique, underwater area. It contains active volcanoes, vents that bubble up liquid sulfur and carbon dioxide, creatures that survive in the deepest depths, and, unfortunately, trash. Scientists discovered a plastic bag as far down as 36,000 feet (10,900 m).

It contained a safety **ballast** balloon, tethered to the sub, that could help steady the sub if needed. Cameron's brain shifted into overdrive. What should he do? Time was ticking. He had reserved the submarine launch ship, the *Mermaid Sapphire*, for only another week and the weather was expected to get worse.

Cameron grabbed his radio control. It was now or never. "Cut it away," he called to his team. "I'm going to dive without it."[1]

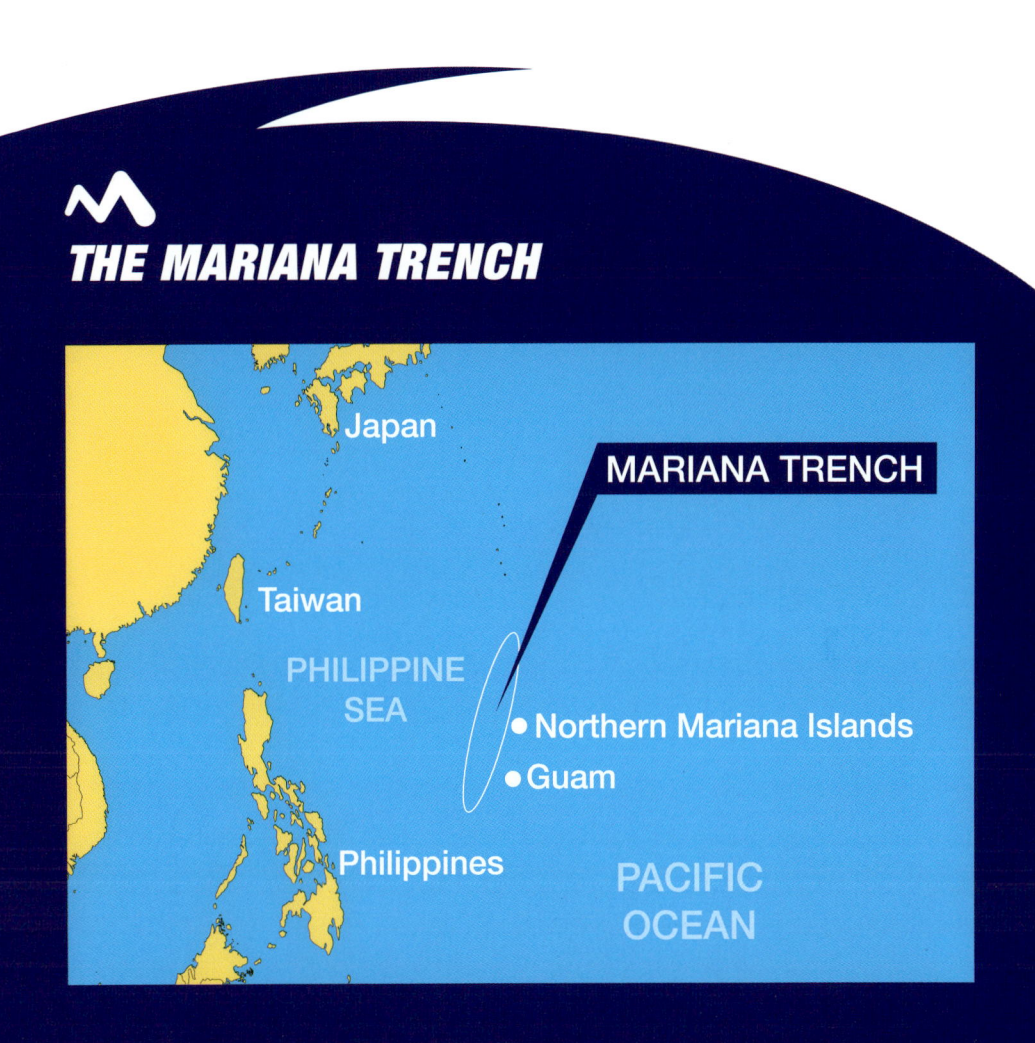

THE MARIANA TRENCH

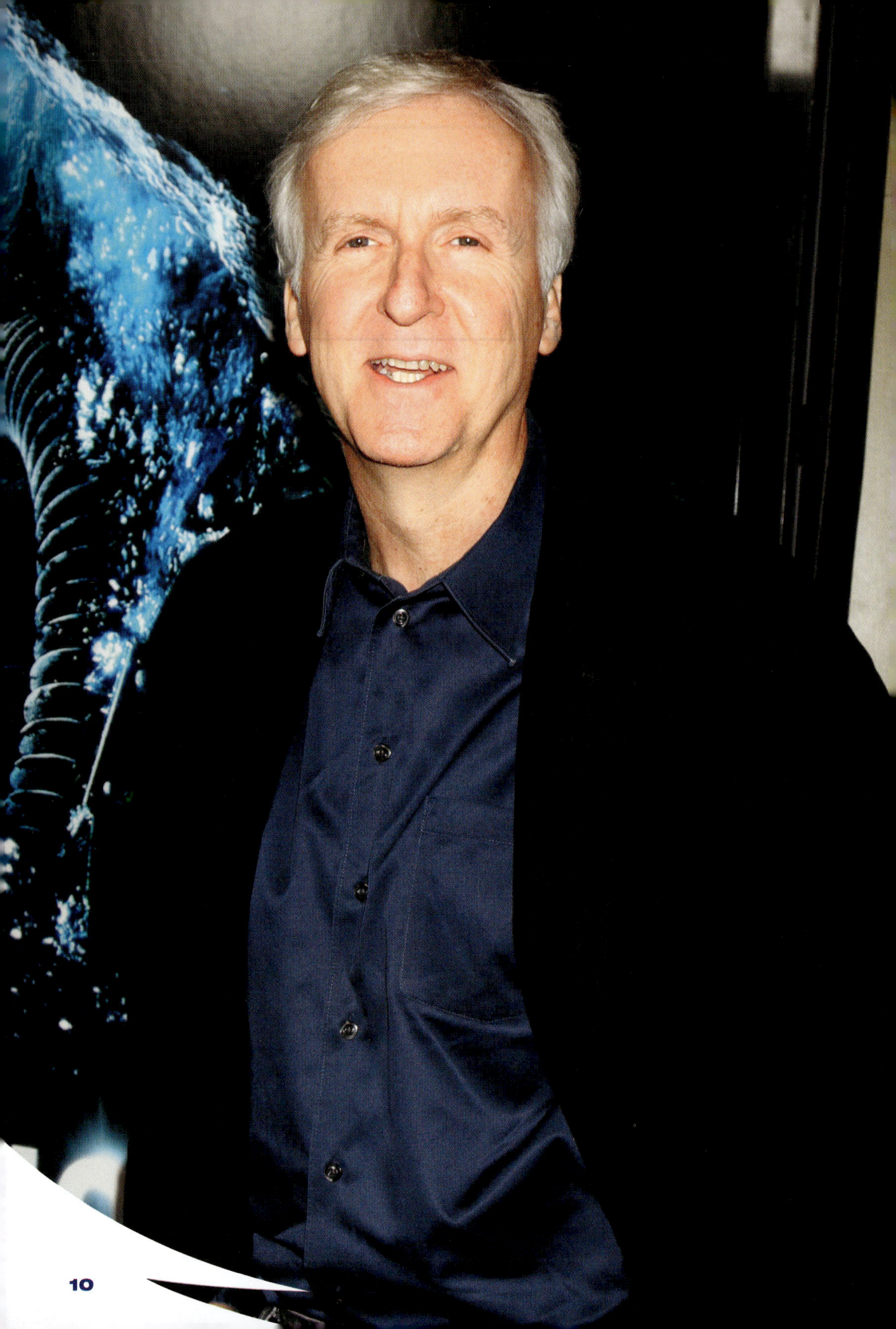

CHAPTER TWO

TEAMWORK

In 2002, while spending long days at sea directing a documentary about a sunken battleship, Cameron shared his childhood dream of building a high-tech submarine with his friend and technical assistant, Ron Allum. Cameron was excited about the idea. He wanted to solo pilot a sub to the deepest part of the ocean. He had been inspired by a 1960 voyage to the bottom of the Challenger Deep in a sub called *Trieste*. Two people had piloted that sub.

Cameron appreciated Allum's brilliance as a problem solver. By the end of 2005, Cameron asked Allum to build his dream sub, and Allum agreed. Cameron wanted his sub to have 3-D cameras; high-powered lights; robotic arms that could collect soil, water, and rock samples; and a device for sucking up tiny creatures. The *Trieste* pilots didn't collect samples or shoot video.

◀ **Cameron is an award-winning director.**

They also stayed on the bottom for only 20 minutes. Cameron hoped to explore the bottom for hours.

Allum spent months developing a new type of foam for the sub's frame. The foam could withstand the crushing water pressure of the deep ocean. By 2011, the *Deepsea Challenger* team included more than 100 engineers, scientists, educators, journalists, and filmmakers. Cameron joined the team in Australia. They held intense strategy meetings and tested each of the sub's parts.

Around the same time, other engineering teams announced that they were working on subs to pilot to the bottom of the Challenger Deep, too: Virgin Oceanic, DOER Marine, and Triton Submarines. Which team's sub would make it to the bottom first?

Cameron's sub was farthest along, but still, the *Deepsea Challenger* engineers discovered problems and weaknesses. Areas of the sub shrank differently under intense water pressure.

FORMATION OF THE CHALLENGER DEEP

The Challenger Deep was formed when two **tectonic plates** collided, in a process called subduction. During this process, the lighter crust plunges into Earth's **mantle** under the heavier crust. This creates a deep ocean trench.

▲ **The *Trieste* had practice dives in various places, including the Mediterranean Sea and the Pacific Ocean.**

The pilot sphere window kept cracking within its steel frame. They tested, redesigned, and retested every piece of the sub over and over again.

Finally, in January 2012, the team loaded up the sub on a big truck and hauled it to the Sydney Naval Dockyards. They planned to test it in the ocean up to a dozen times, starting in the shallower waters of Jervis Bay. Then, in late March, Cameron would make the big dive to the deepest depths of the ocean, to the bottom of the Challenger Deep. He could hardly wait.

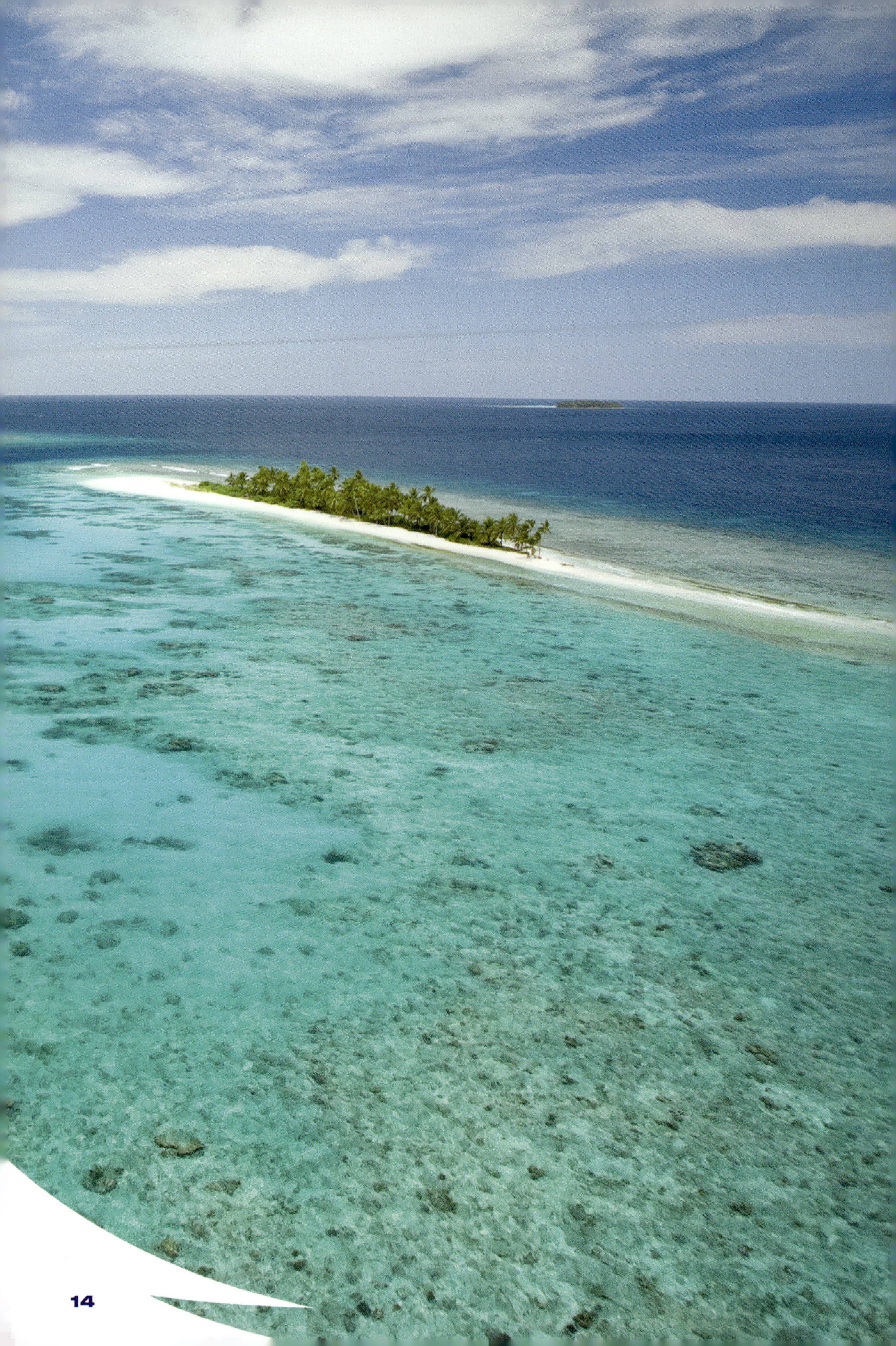

CHAPTER THREE

A RACE FOR TIME

In February 2012, an early test dive for the *Deepsea Challenger* was about to begin. Just as the crane was hoisting the sub over the water, Cameron radioed Allum and said, "Abort the dive."[2]

Cameron shared the terrible news that two *Deepsea Challenger* teammates, Andrew Wight and Mike deGruy, both filmmakers, had just died in a helicopter crash. The team was devastated. They considered canceling the entire voyage. But after two weeks of grieving, they decided to continue on.

In the waters near Papua New Guinea, the team experienced more difficulties. From the minute the sub hit the water, with Cameron piloting, everything went haywire. The electrical system flashed on and off. The device that absorbs excess carbon dioxide fell off the wall of the pilot sphere onto Cameron's lap. The 3-D cameras didn't work. Cameron called off the dive.

◀ **Papua New Guinea has many islands.**

▲ **Cameron sat in a pilot sphere model to show people its size.**

Later, after a lot of problem-solving and hard work, the team achieved some success. Cameron piloted the sub down to 3,280 feet (1,000 m), where he spent three hours in awe looking at eels, strange-looking sea cucumbers, and other creatures. "After the loss of Andrew and Mike," Cameron said, "we needed a comeback. We needed a win. Tonight we got it."[3]

Cameron's team was far ahead of the other teams by this time. Virgin Oceanic's sleek, airplane-shaped sub was not ready to test in deep water. And the designs for the other two teams' subs were still on the drawing board.

Soon after his 3,280-foot (1,000-m) dive, Cameron made it down to 23,818 feet (7,260 m) in the New Britain Trench near Papua New Guinea. He felt that he had made excellent progress. But the *Deepsea Challenger*'s software had a glitch, forcing him to return to the surface earlier than he expected. There were only a few test dives to go to fix all the problems.

The stormy weather was not making their dives easy. Cameron and his team canceled several more dives. "Now we've got no choice but to run right up to our deadline," Cameron said, pacing the launch ship deck.[4] There would be no more test dives. He would have to make the big dive soon. The morning of March 26, during a window of calmer weather, Cameron and his team decided to go for it. There was no time to lose.

NEW DISCOVERIES

During test dives in the New Britain Trench at 26,902 feet (8,200 m), Cameron's team discovered foot-long, shrimp-like creatures. These pale, never-seen-before *amphipods* contain a substance also found in coconut palms. The substance is being studied to potentially treat Alzheimer's disease, a common form of **dementia**.

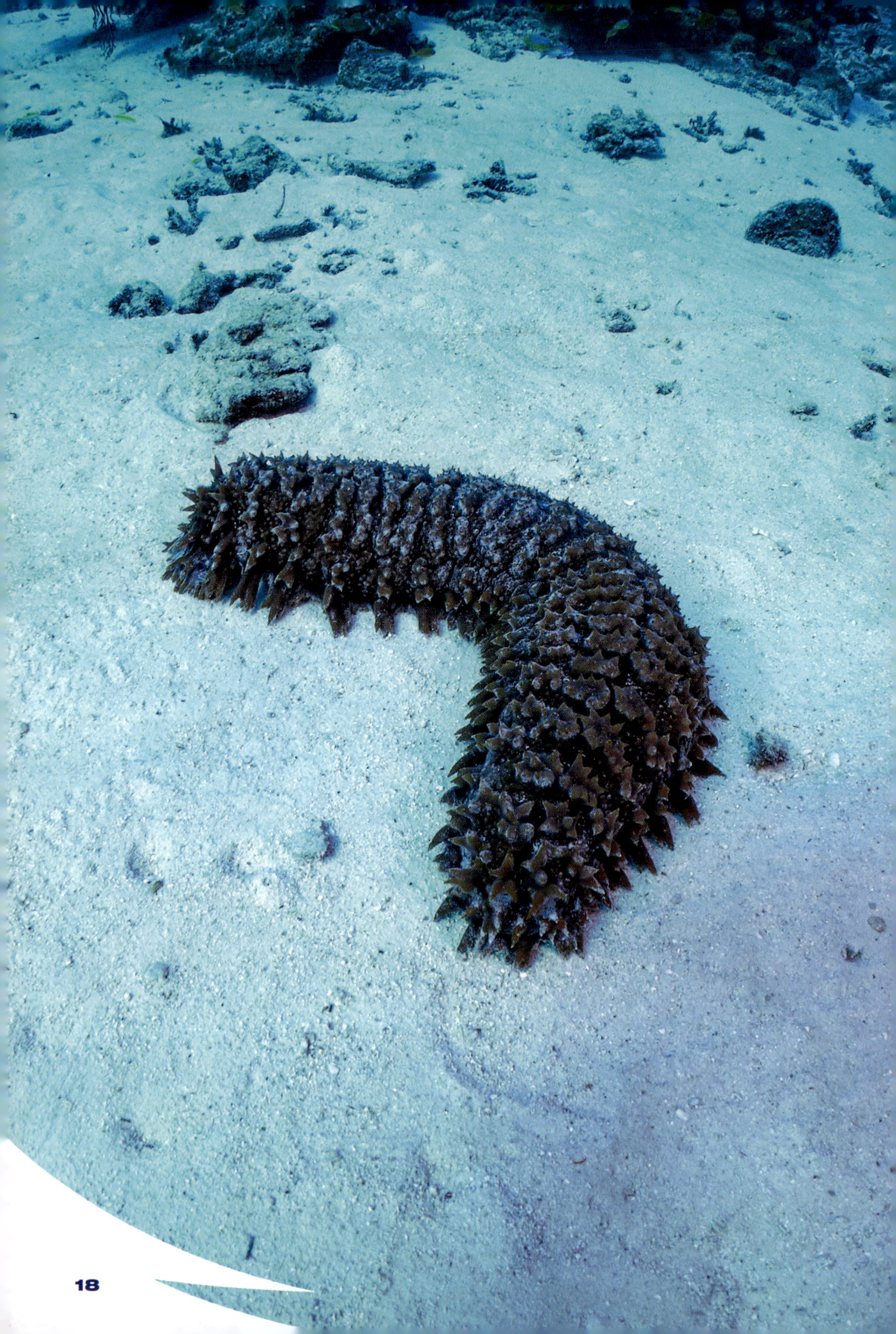

CHAPTER FOUR

THE BIG DIVE

Cameron waited as crew members cut away the hatch and the safety ballast balloon. While the sub pitched and tossed in the waves, he sat tucked into the Deepsea Challenger's pilot sphere. Cameron said later that he felt like, "a walnut in its shell."[5] Nearly 7 miles (11 km) below lay the bottom of the Challenger Deep. As soon as they finished, Cameron took a deep breath and radioed his crew: "OK, ready to initiate **descent**. And release, release, release!"[6]

Flooded with adrenaline, Cameron's worries floated away. The pilot sphere was packed with navigation controls, cameras, and other electronics. He knew how to use every piece of equipment. He was ready.

The sub sank down at nearly 500 feet (152 m) per minute. Slowly, Cameron powered up the systems listed on his checklist.

◀ **Sea cucumbers live in the Mariana Trench.**

He didn't want the pilot sphere to get too hot from starting up the systems all at once. "I'd bake," Cameron explained later. "I'd literally be like a poached salmon."[7]

Soon, the water temperature fell from 85 degrees Fahrenheit (29°C) at the surface to 35 degrees Fahrenheit (1.6°C). **Condensation** dripped on Cameron's head. He put on wool socks, waterproof booties, and a knit cap. Even though the water was completely dark, he saw plankton rush up through the sub's light beams like flurries of snow.

With 9,000 feet (2,740 m) to go and his checklist complete, Cameron thought about the intense water pressure pushing against the outside of the sub. If the sub cracked, even a little, the pilot sphere would buckle and he would die.

Finally, after another hour, with only 150 feet (45 m) left to go until he reached the bottom, Cameron operated the controls that released steel ball bearings from the sub. This made the sub lighter. Without the extra weight, the *Deepsea Challenger* slowed. It eased toward the bottom.

The two landing feet sank into the fine **silt**, and his journey down was complete. "Surface, this is *Deepsea Challenger,*" Cameron radioed. "I am on the bottom. . . . Life support's good, everything looks good."[8]

Cameron has been involved in many different ▶ projects, including space exploration.

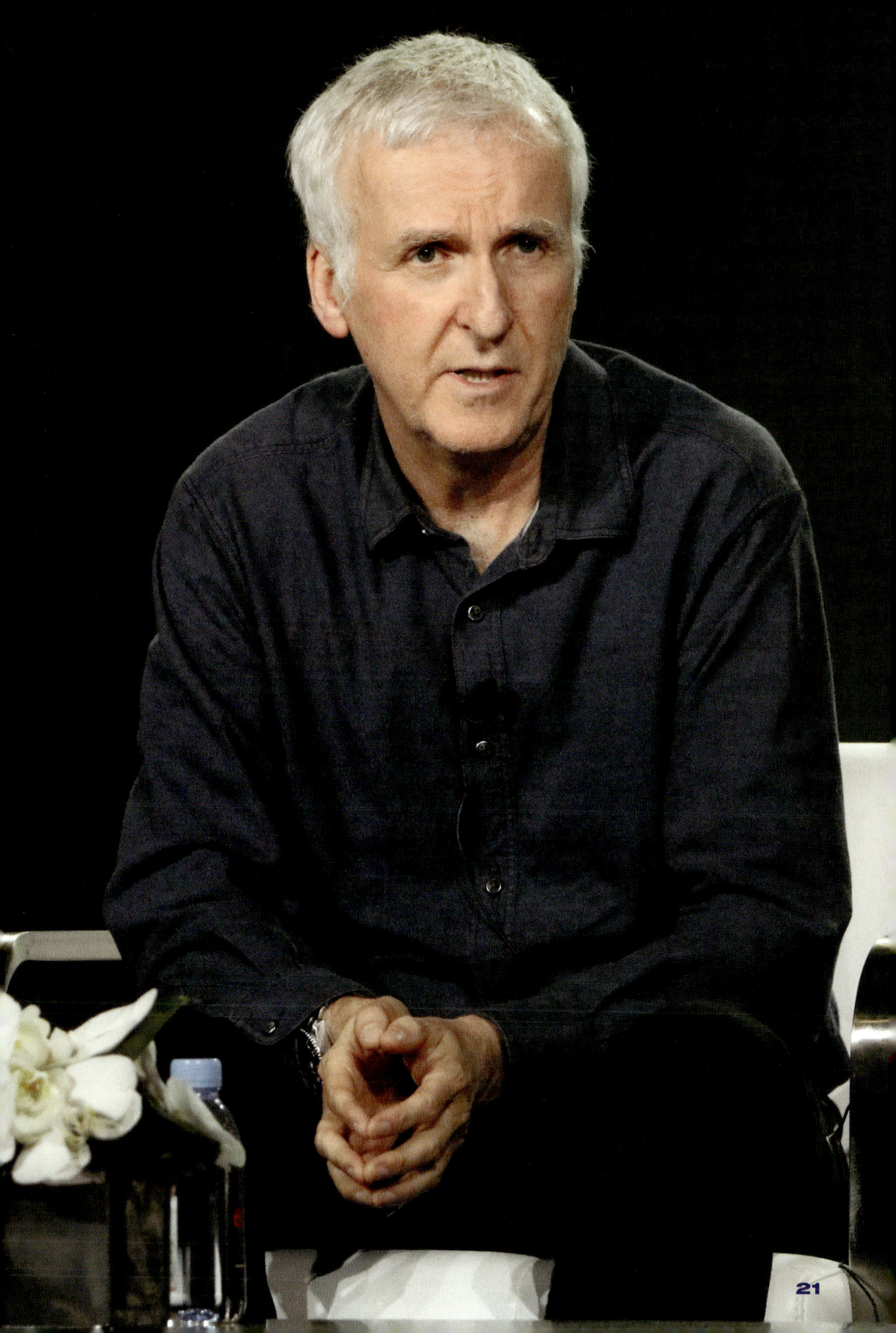

▲ **Cameron showed off a scale model of the *Deepsea Challenger* to the media.**

To Cameron's surprise, he didn't see much. He later said it looked like "a parking lot covered with new fallen snow . . . pretty much the bleakest place I had ever seen in the ocean."[9] Another time he described it as "a completely alien world."[10] The dark, cold water and extreme pressure is too much for most living things.

After gazing into the vastness for a few moments, Cameron started up the robotic arm. He used it to gather a mud sample.

But before he could collect more samples, Cameron saw that something was wrong with a system, and the robotic arm would soon stop working.

With no way to collect more samples, but with cameras still working, Cameron decided to explore. He started up the thrusters. The sub moved slowly across the ocean floor. He steered it toward the wall of the trench, hoping to encounter rock outcroppings.

About 1 mile (1.6 km) from his landing site, however, his compass was having some problems. Then, several of his batteries became dangerously low, and some of the thrusters failed. Cameron struggled to control the sub. It lurched to the right, then another thruster failed. He could only turn the sub in circles. What next?

Cameron had hoped to stay on the bottom for five hours, collecting samples and shooting video and pictures. He'd only been there for around three hours. Still, he figured he was better safe than sorry. He would abort his mission early.

Cameron flipped the switch to release two 536-pound (243-kg) weights that would allow the sub to go to the surface. He worried they wouldn't drop, but then he heard the weights slide down their tracks and sink to the ocean floor. Cameron sighed with relief.

▲ **A ghost fish was seen in the Mariana Trench. This rare fish doesn't have any color because it lives deep in the ocean.**

The sub lurched, then rose toward the surface, rocking back and forth as it gained speed.

The crew of the support helicopter spotted the sub first, once it emerged from the water. Before long, a crane aboard the *Mermaid Sapphire* lifted the *Deepsea Challenger* back onto the ship. Cameron's team, who had spent so much time and effort making this day happen, clapped and cheered. Safely on deck, Cameron grinned.

THE TWO SUBS IN THE CHALLENGER DEEP

1960: *Trieste*	2012: *Deepsea Challenger*
Weighed 150 tons (136,000 kg)	Weighed 11.8 tons (10,700 kg)
The *Trieste* needed two pilots to operate it.	The *Deepsea Challenger* needed one pilot to operate it.
It took four hours and 48 minutes to get to the bottom.	It took about two hours and 30 minutes to get to the bottom.
It took about three hours and 15 minutes to come back to the surface.	It took about 70 minutes to come back to the surface.
The *Trieste* couldn't take photos.	The *Deepsea Challenger* had eight cameras, a mechanical arm to pick up things outside the submarine, a device to test the water, and more.
The *Trieste* was at the bottom for 20 minutes.	The *Deepsea Challenger* was at the bottom for around three hours.

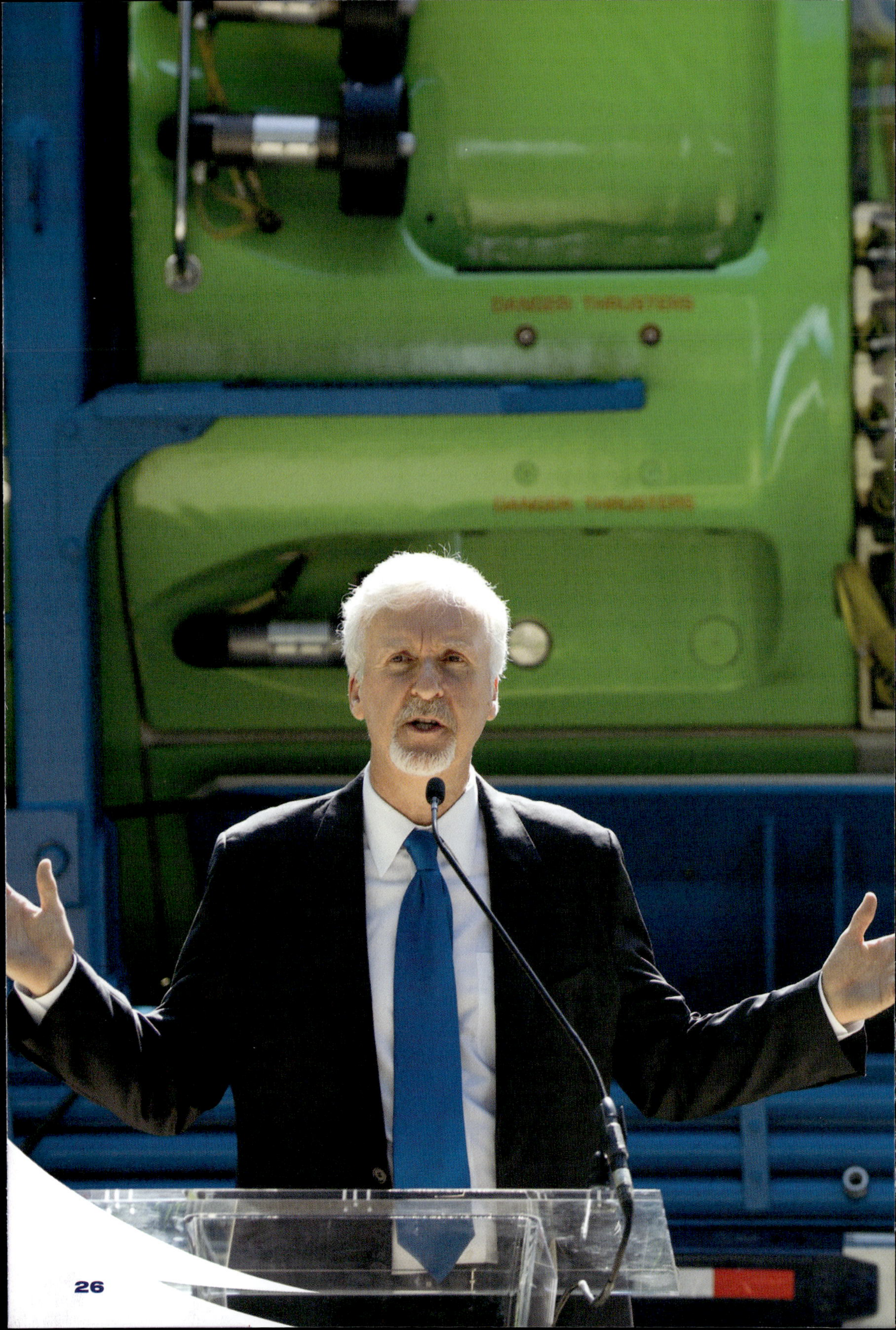
DANGER THRUSTERS
DANGER THRUSTERS

CHAPTER FIVE

THE JOURNEY CONTINUES

Cameron spoke to a group of excited middle schoolers and onlookers on June 14, 2013. "Follow your curiosity and the things that interest you," he said.[11] The *Deepsea Challenger*, which Cameron was donating to the Woods Hole Oceanographic Institution (WHOI) in Massachusetts that day, loomed behind him.

Cameron hoped the new technology he developed for his sub, such as its high-definition cameras, flotation systems, and energy storage and lighting systems, would be incorporated into other deep-sea vehicles and inspire future deep-sea journeys. As of 2018, no one besides Cameron and the *Trieste* pilots have driven a sub to the bottom of the Challenger Deep. The Virgin Oceanic team halted progress on their sub in 2014, and the DOER Marine and Triton Submarines teams are still working on theirs.

◀ After his dive, Cameron showed off his sub to the public.

▲ **There are thousands of species of** *amphipods.*

Besides donating his sub to WHOI, Cameron has contributed to the scientific community in other ways. After carefully examining his high-definition videos and mud sample, scientists were thrilled to discover 68 new species, including several semitransparent, crayon-sized sea cucumbers. These creatures lay on the sea floor, collecting food with their tentacles. They also discovered *xenophyophores* that looked like giant **amoebas** and tiny, shrimp-like *amphipods.*

Scientists also discovered new types of bacteria. They hope that by learning more about how these bacteria get their food, they will better understand how life began on Earth.

Cameron released his documentary, *James Cameron's Deepsea Challenge 3D*, in 2014. He wanted to boost people's interest in the deep oceans and inspire government officials to fund future journeys. In 2019, Cameron was busy making movies. But someday he plans to sink back down to the deepest depths and peer out of the pilot sphere window once again.

THINK ABOUT IT

▶ Why do you think Cameron put in so much of his own time to develop the *Deepsea Challenger*?
▶ Why do you think more people haven't explored the Challenger Deep?
▶ What surprises you the most about life at the bottom of the deepest oceans?

GLOSSARY

amoebas (uh-MEE-buhz): Amoebas are single-celled organisms that engulf other microorganisms for food. Amoebas thrive in the ocean and in freshwater.

ballast (BAL-uhst): Ballast is a heavy material that provides stability. The *Deepsea Challenger* had a safety ballast balloon.

condensation (kahn-den-SAY-shun): Condensation is water droplets that collect on a cold surface from contact with humid air. Condensation dripped on Cameron while he was in the submarine.

dementia (dih-MEN-shuh): Dementia is a brain disorder that causes memory problems, changes in personality, and difficulty with reasoning. Alzheimer's disease is a common form of dementia.

descent (di-SENT): Descent means to move from a higher place to a lower place. Cameron was ready for his submarine to make its descent into the ocean.

mantle (MAN-tuhl): The mantle is the area on Earth between the planet's core and crust. Crust on Earth will sometimes be pushed into Earth's mantle.

silt (SILT): Silt is fine sand or organic matter. The submarine landed in silt.

sphere (SFEER): A sphere is a round enclosure. The pilot of the submarine squeezed into a small pilot sphere.

tectonic plates (tek-TAHN-ik PLAYTZ): Tectonic plates are large sections in Earth's crust that move. The Challenger Deep was formed when tectonic plates collided.

SOURCE NOTES

1. Bruce Barcott. "Voyage to the Deep." *National Geographic*. National Geographic Society, June 2013. Web. 15 Jan. 2019.

2. Ibid.

3. Ibid.

4. Ibid.

5. James Cameron. "Pressure Dive." *National Geographic*. National Geographic Society, June 2013. Web. 15 Jan. 2019.

6. Ibid.

7. Larry Greenemeier. "Deep Thoughts: James Cameron on the New Age of Exploration and His 11-Kilometer Dive to the Challenger Deep, Part 1." *Scientific American*. Scientific American, 30 May 2013. Web. 15 Jan. 2019.

8. James Cameron. "Pressure Dive." *National Geographic*. National Geographic Society, June 2013. Web. 15 Jan. 2019.

9. Carolyn Giardina. "'Deepsea Challenge 3D': The Story Behind James Cameron's Dive to the Mariana Trench." *Hollywood Reporter*. Hollywood Reporter, 6 Aug. 2014. Web. 15 Jan. 2019.

10. William J. Broad. "At Bottom of Pacific, Director Sees Dark Frontier." *New York Times*. New York Times Company, 26 Mar. 2012. Web. 15 Jan. 2019.

11. Douglas Main. "James Cameron Gives Record-Breaking Sub to Science." *Live Science*. Live Science, 14 June 2013. Web. 15 Jan. 2019.

TO LEARN MORE

BOOKS

Spilsbury, Richard. *Robots Underwater.* New York, NY: Gareth Stevens Publishing, 2016.

Wilsdon, Christina. *Ultimate Oceanpedia: The Most Complete Ocean Reference Ever.* Washington, DC: National Geographic Children's Books, 2016.

Woodward, John. *Ocean: A Visual Encyclopedia.* New York, NY: DK Publishing, 2015.

WEBSITES

Visit our website for links about the race to the bottom of the ocean: **childsworld.com/links**

Note to Parents, Teachers, and Librarians: We routinely verify our Web links to make sure they are safe and active sites. So encourage your readers to check them out!

INDEX

Challenger Deep, 4, 7, 11–13, 19, 27

Deepsea Challenger, 4, 7–8, 12, 15, 17, 19–20, 24, 27

Mariana Trench, 4, 7–8

pilot sphere, 7, 13, 15, 19–20, 29

robotic arm, 11, 22–23

safety ballast balloon, 9, 19

sea cucumbers, 16, 28

Trieste, 4, 11, 27

Triton Submarines, 12, 27

Virgin Oceanic, 12, 16, 27

water pressure, 4, 7, 12, 20